Parenting
INSPIRED

Parenting INSPIRED

Follow the Path,
Where the Child Loves to Grow

HANIFA K. COOK

PARTRIDGE

ISBN: Softcover   978-1-4828-6385-7
             eBook   978-1-4828-6386-4

To order additional copies of this book, contact
Toll Free 800 101 2657 (Singapore)
Toll Free 1 800 81 7340 (Malaysia)
orders.singapore@partridgepublishing.com

www.partridgepublishing.com/singapore

Dedication

To my wonderful husband Steve
You are where my heart is, at home.
To my daughter, Jazima
I am so proud to be your mother.

Acknowledgements

There are so many people to thank for this journey. At the time of writing this book, I was nearing my 50th birthday and have spent 15 years as a mother. I also have nearly 50 years of experience using 4 languages and have used that experience in personal development for parenting and business.

I want to thank my dear husband. You have shown me the way to think with my heart and feel with my mind. The woman does things in the opposite. So having you as a partner in life is a true blessing. You have helped me clarify my doubts that my heart is in sync with my thoughts. Home is where the heart is. With you, I always feel at home.

To my daugher, the pearl of my eyes and the star of my parenthood journey. You have piggybacked me from the time you were born. In my most fragile moments, you called my name and never stopped wanting me to find the strength to get up and become the parent. You have taught me a lot. Thank you for sharing your space with us. This book tells you how much you have inspired me.

I want to thank members of my Facebook group "iPostForParents", some of whom have contributed to this book. You have stayed up late to read my posts and walked with me on this journey. This book is testimony to my work and we can now use it together. http://www.facebook.com/groups/ipostforparents.

To my students and their parents. I am so proud to teach you and see you grow. There are so many incredible achievements. I thank the parents for trusting me with the work of helping your children to grow confident and become successful. And also for collaborating with me to facilitate for your children's growth.

To my friends and family members, thank you for your prayers and continued support.

To my mother, Hamidah Masagos Omar and father, Allahyarham Kahar bin Sokijo. You have inspired me to look at parenting in a special way. You gave me the opportunity to grow and get an education. I can never match up to you dedication. Your love and devotion are the reasons why I can complete this book with pride.

Hanifa K. Cook

Foreword

Finally, a book that captures the essence of about how to follow our children's growth. It is written for the parent by a parent. The personal recounts will resonate with many women and men who are entering parenthood. Hanifa has allowed herself to be the focus of attention in order to explore the behaviour and love of growing up in children.

She summarises these explorations and findings clearly in this book. She has religiously followed her own inner teacher and has herself been inspired. The inspired parent follows a very simple rule, follow the child. How easy it should be, yet we have not given this #followthechild concept much thought. We think it will work better for us if we thought of parenting the other way around. That is for the child to follow the adult.

Indeed, we are inspired by the child. We have created the facilities and learning environment for the child because the child wishes to grow. If inspiration does not lead us to the child, we might as well have stayed ignorant and we shall remain uninformed and uneducated. If we are only inspired to provide by what we have, within limits of our resources, there will be a disconnection between the facilitators and the child.

What is even more admirable is that Hanifa demonstrates to us what every parent struggles with every day. How do you find a balance in our life at work, in business and with the family? You will read that her courage is the same courage we all have, yet she has used that courage in the direction that works for both herself and her child.

I am grateful that with each passing day, I am always surrounded by the care and love of my wife and children. Our hectic schedules have often left us barely enough time to gather the entire family on special occasions, birthdays, anniversaries and even funerals.

There are many books about parenting on the market. One that takes you and pulls you by the hand don't come in a book like this. If you have been pondering over this subject, parenting and how to follow the child, then you have to take this book with you in your parenthood journey.

Sani Hamid
Proud parent of two young boys
& Director, Economy & Market Strategy, Wealth Management
Financial Alliance Private Limited

More About The Book

Hello there! Ever since I was little, I have always known I can easily discern intonation and modulation of language sounds. This means I can articulate and pronounce words with ease. So for nearly 50 years, I have been speaking four languages. I am a polyglot. This book is a collection of my motherhood constellations based on my parenting experience and working with parents for the last 15 years.

We often take for granted that after having children, we can apply the skills and knowledge our parents have taught us. If only it was that simple, there would be a template for parents to fill in before we left the hospitals with our babies.

In this book, you will learn how to use the basic principles of Montessori philosophies about children. I have outlined the love characteristics of children which have proven to be priceless gems. If you are not sure what children are made of, you will find these so easy to follow and understand.

Combined with simple strategies in personal development, you can apply these philosophies to follow your child and grow as a team. Building a family takes faith, trust and a lot of sacrifices. Sometimes, you want to give up because the road to adulthood from babyhood seems so long. I was like many parents before me. I had cried lots of tears till my daughter had to tell daddy to come and fix me. I could see that my daughter is a gift from up above, and that instantly took me out of the rut.

First, I was raised in a multicultural and multiracial society. This largely formed the background of how I became a polyglot. When my daughter turned 3 years of age, my first concern was therefore whether I could guide her to learn all the non-native languages. Why did I worry? That is because learning and teaching are two different matters. They require two different mindsets.

Second, I raised my daughter to speak 3 languages when it was impossible to get resources freely. There was not much on the internet to work from. We lived in Jakarta during the first 6 years of my daughter's life. The Chinese language was only taught at private or international schools.

Finally, I am neither a native Chinese nor English speaker. I take pride in accomplishing a complex task, teaching my daughter to speak 3 languages within the first 6 years of her life.

My parenting journey has taken me through many phases, academically and professionally. If you are working towards connecting with your child and still run your business, work and family, this book will support you in this journey.

I have successfully used my gift of speech as a mast when I set sail on this parenting journey. Welcome on board this ship. All aboard! Ahoy!

Parenthood is the journey, childhood is the ride.

Contents

PART THREE

PART FOUR

PART FIVE

Introduction
To Childhoodspeech™?

In 2008, I created a blog called http://www.childhoodspeech.com. In the beginning, I wrote my blogs to make sense of my journey as a parent. It gave me that sense of fulfilment and influenced me to be stable and calm. At that time, it was an expedition, into the world of childhood. Blogging helped me to build my credentials and deepen my knowledge about teaching children, most importantly my daughter.

As I continued to blog, money became less attractive than the desire to understand more about raising a multilingual child who is resilient, independent and resourceful. I started to dive deep into the subject of childhood experiences and development. Every night, after I finished teaching online, I looked at my daughter who was fast asleep beside me. It was 2 a.m. She had to get ready for the school bus at 6 a.m. I managed to put her through kindergarten somehow. Kindergarten? It was not that hard, was it? It was. It is one of those stories which has made an impact in my parenting journey. You shall be reading about it in one of the chapters.

I have written over 300 articles online. The blog continues to stay on the number 1 spot on search engine results. More importantly, I manage to document my thoughts about raising a multilingual child and the subject of the parenting. My work, as a blogger then, brought me stability as a parent and kept me grounded academically and intellectually. In 2015, I published my first chapter entitled "Remembering Childhood Speech Constantly" in a bestselling book anthology "Born For This! The Journey to Success in Life, Love and Business". My work has also gained lots of interests with educators, so much so that I am invited to give motivational talks to parents and students in schools. Today, you are holding a book that has taken me 15 years to prepare, and perhaps 7 years to write. I am indeed grateful that I am now able to share Childhoodspeech™ with you. So thank you for picking up this book.

Although there are several books on the subject of parenting, I cannot find one that can help me bridge the gap between the adult and the child. Generally speaking, the parent is asked to understand the child. At the same time, the child is expected to model after the parent.

My daughter and I were on a spinning wheel, locked in this cycle of life. I want more than just being inside this spinning wheel. I know there is a valve which needs to be filled and a bridge to be built. I found new answers when I started digging deep into my own childhood. I discovered that all strengths and weaknesses that we revealed in our childhood become the true foundations of our future success and happiness. So many famous figures always talk about how they have been brought up as part of their success stories. Needless to mention, when someone becomes famous, the first thing you want to find out about them is their background. I become more and more certain that in order for me to be a better parent and live a happy and successful life as an adult, I need to study Childhoodspeech™.

One of the unsuspecting perils of becoming an adult is that the adult tends to speak of childhood experiences as if they are hidden memories from the past. The problem is when it is time to celebrate birthdays, Christmas, Aidul Fitiri, Lunar New Year, Deepavali, and so forth, the adults find themselves reliving childhood memories. It seems to me that we are living in denial. As a matter of fact, the cycle of life continues to spin in the same direction, from childhood to adulthood and so it goes. The child becomes the adult parent who in turn raises children of his or her own. The cakes, cookies, festive fashions, decorations and so forth always make their way back into the cycle. People remember how it was like to be a child again, holding their parents' hands as they make their way to their grandparents homes for the family gathering. A friend of mine has kept her mother's Christmas tree for 15 years. Indeed, childhood experiences are not hidden memories; they are treasures.

Every adult has come from the child. Besides this, the emotions, troubles, failures and successes, that we bring along from our childhood will make a difference to our lives as adults. In other words, if we want to raise a child who owns the qualities and characteristics of a strong adult, we have to start talking about childhood with more earnest and great intent. We need to define what childhood means, not what it is. We need to know about who we are as children, not who we once were as kids. We must not hold back on discussing our childhood experiences because they are bad experiences and then spend many nights alone in the dark crying for the hugs of our parents.

As we start to discuss parenting, we usually do not know when and where to begin. We therefore categorically place the child on the timeline: 0-6 years old, 6-12 years old, 13-18 years old and so forth. The kids are grouped based on their ages for purpose of convenience. This is called vertical classification. It is unfortunate because adults who share their childhood experiences don't relate memories with their age, but with a period in their lives. Age is not the matter for discussion. Childhood is a period in the life of every individual. Thus, parenting styles will continue to be shaped by the way you have been brought up.

How can this book help you think about childhood as a period and part of the total sum of age groups at different phases in your child's growth? I have organised the chapters into the love characteristics of children. These love characteristics are easily recognisable and identifiable even in the most awkward situations like when the child smears paint all over the body. In addition to this, I give personal recounts on how I came to discover these characteristics from my experience.

Generally speaking, Childhoodspeech™ has adopted the philosophical theories of Maria Montessori[1], a famous lady who studied and worked with children. Montessori's philosophies about childhood development sit comfortably with my parenting styles. As I fuse these two components over the last 15 years, I develop Childhoodspeech™ into a full practical guide for parents. The intention is to unlock the secrets to living up to our parenting, with an appreciation for childhood.

As a parent, I do not see thee child's age as a simple measure of growth to be put on a timeline or to be classified to aid education. As the child grows, the physical changes, character development and brain works are the mainstay in childhood experiences. Leave the classification of the child by age to the system of education. Pre-school, high school, college and then university. There are plenty of references to help parents to plan for education. Only when there is no education available, then there is a reason to worry. As parents, our first business is to provide for the child not by age or physical change but by virtue. The parent should not have to figure out what and how to treat the child at different phases of growth just because there is a study about early childhood development or a new development in medicine to treat teenage depression. A child is a child. We should not over complicate the work of the child nor overburden our role as the parent. Accept the journey of parenthood as it unfolds together with childhood. Neither you nor your spouse will have to bear the guilt of not having done enough because we are not comparing our children with studies and findings.

---

[1]   Maria Montessori, https://en.wikipedia.org/wiki/Maria_Montessori

How To Begin With Childhoodspeech™

I recommend that you complete the following exercise first. It is quite simply an exercise to orientate you to childhood, a phase in our lives that we might have forgotten or left behind a long time ago.

Answer this about your childhood.

1. What is your relationship with your childhood?
   Proceed to the page xxi to write about what your childhood.

Answer this question about your childbirth experience **if you have a child**.

2. Pick one moment when you first saw your baby up close. Perhaps when you were feeding, changing the diapers or stroking the baby's forehead as you admired the beauty of a newborn. Describe that feeling and remember how it happened.

Place your right palm close to your heart. Feel your heartbeat. Start breathing slowly. Remember and recall, you are listening to your little baby's heartbeat. You are carrying your baby for the first time. The baby's neck is resting firmly on your left hand. Your palm gently cups its small, delicate bottom. Through the warmth of the towel, you could feel your baby snuggling deeper and deeper into the palm of your hand.

You hold your child so close to you that you can smell the skin through the soft cotton fabric that wraps the tiny little body. You hold your child gently. Your baby is so fragile and delicate that you dare breathe but softly, afraid to wake the baby up. You have remembered that you have washed your hands. So you confidently bend your head down to kiss the little fingers. You can see the baby's lips open slightly and then they close again.

Your baby's eyes open slightly. Your baby's tiny fingers grip onto your pinky finger. You reach down again and kiss the cheeks. The soft skin of your lips now touching your baby's cheek.

Think of 3 words to describe how you feel about this experience. When you have 3 words, open your eyes, write what your heart says about your baby.

When did parenting actually begin for you? And why do you think that is the beginning of your parenting journey. Fill in the next page with what you can see, feel, smell and touch in this experience. This is the center from where your love and affection resides. This is the place of energy that binds the relationship between you and your child. This is important to always go back to these experiences before we make any new decisions that might affect our lives. What the baby has given us is a reason to live, thereupon we embark on a journey into parenthood. Let's begin.

Write Three Words That Describes Your Childhood Or Your Baby

I see:

1.

I feel:

2.

I smell:

3.

I hear:

4.

I give thanks to:

5.

PART ONE

Revisiting Childbirth, How My Parenting Begins

If you were with me on 5th November 2001, you would have seen me sitting in the hall waiting for my final examination. I heard my name being called out, "HANIFA!" It was so loud that it startled me. As I picked up my heavy body, my butt slid across the plastic seat as it was too low for me to get up. "Stupid nurse! Is this the way to treat a pregnant lady?" I gave her a quick stare as I walked pass her.

Stepping onto the small stool to get on the bed to be examined, my legs felt wobbly and my body suddenly felt really heavy. I went blank for a moment. Dizzy. My thighs felt wet. I was sweating. I felt water trickling down my thighs, it felt dense but warm. I gasped at the thought of having to go through this one more time. Last checkup. After this, the baby will be out of this body. "Gasp!" Blood. It was not perspiration. It was my blood.

"Help me," I called out faintly, feeling helpless at the sight of my own blood. "Help me, please!" I called out louder. The curtain swung open. "Yes?" The room was very small. My back was facing her, so she has to squeeze to get to see what I was pointing to. "Help." I pointed to the floor. I lifted up my blouse. A puddle of blood had already collected in my underwear.

If you were with me, you would have seen me standing there on a stool, looking down at the blood on my feet and all over my thighs. The nurses frantically gave me several tissue papers. Blood had already collected in my underwear. I wondered if they knew what they were doing. "Crap!" I had to get rid of everything I was wearing. Into the garbage bag the clothing went. I remember feeling really cold. They gave me new clothing from the hospital and gently got me to sit me in a wheelchair. This time, I was told to move slowly. Too late, the damage had already been done.

In the emergency room, at least 10 people darted in and out to prepare for the emergency caesarian. The drip, consent form, injections, temperature check and blood pressure checks. "We cannot find the heartbeat madam." I waited and calmly tried to breathe slower. I know it was there, I needed to calm down. It felt like forever. The baby's heartbeat finally came through on the machine. Everyone who had stopped to listen for it sprang back into action. The surgeon finally entered the room. He said, "You have tried. It (dilation) was about 4 cm. Let's get the baby out now. You are going to be fine." My husband was overseas at this point in time. I made a quick phone call to inform him about it.

This was not the first time I had bled. I was only three weeks pregnant when it was discovered then that I had a very low placenta. By the end of my pregnancy, I had low placenta previa[2]. C-section was not an option; it was the only choice. Emergency caesarian was certainly not what we had planned for, though.

When I came around after surgery, my whole body shivered uncontrollably. It was hell! I kept calling out for help, faintly. But I only heard this, "We have already done our best for her. Now it is up to her." I wanted to cry, but I couldn't. Whenever I recall that moment right after surgery, I am disgusted by the way I was treated. I don't remember what happened next. I must have passed out. I woke up in the ward; I had been given morphine.

---

[2] Placenta previa: a condition in which the placenta partially or wholly blocks the neck of the uterus, so interfering with normal delivery of a baby.

Later I heard someone said that I had very low threshold for pain. "What a silly comment!" If you had been carrying a baby for 9 months, you would have been so exhausted by the time the term was over. Let alone a pregnancy with the low placenta and then placenta previa. The placenta was right at the bottom right side of the womb, near to the hip joint.

On the second day, the head nurse asked if I would see a therapist to help me to get out of bed. What? Get up now? Every breath I took hurt. Move?

I thought to myself, "I have yet to feed my daughter. How am I going to look after a baby when I can't even get myself out of bed?!"

When I finally did take my first step away from the bed, I could feel my veins splitting in different directions! It was so scary. My gut was cut open and I had had low placenta previa for 9 months.

My husband had arrived that night after the delivery. The next day, he was there to support me with the therapy session. The therapist showed me how to get out of bed, one arm for support and push, Pilates style. Two feet on the ground and push my body up with two hands. "Keep going. Take another short step. You are doing fine." I yelled out. My screams had gone right through the hallway of the ward. No pain, no gain. I must have benefited a lot from the therapy session because I did get up that night, by myself.

With one deep breath, I tightened my tummy and rolled over to the side of the bed. I managed to walk to the toilet by myself again. This was how my parenting journey began, that one breath, one movement. Can you recall how you began to feel that you are a parent?

Early Independence
Starts At Home

If men of the future are to be strong, they must
be independent and free.[3]

Remember how teachers and parents used to comment our achievements as a kid? We required significant investment and push to figure out how to eat, wash, get dressed and put on shoes with our little fingers. We felt noble, didn't we?

As we grow older, we discover independence. Steadily, learning turns out to be less fascinating. We skip doing a couple of steps, avoiding the simple steps yet driving to stay concentrate on the result. Do you find yourself eating breakfast, drink tea or coffee all at the same time while tying shoelaces at the front door? Have you stood up to drink coffee from a mug, eat cereal in front of lounge room while watching the morning news? After that, you surge off to work, deserting the dishes on the table.

If your routine consists of hurrying off to work every morning, you are forcing your body to work even before leaving the house. By the end of the day, your energy depletes, and you are irate and upset. Why isn't the bed made yet? Where are my socks?

---

[3]   Maria Montessori, The Discovery of the Child, page 58

Adaptation

"We adapt and create new ways to make life better and easier."

We flew to Australia from Singapore with our daughter forty days after the delivery. Two weeks later, we flew to Jakarta where we lived as foreign expatriates for six years.

In Jakarta, I evaded long journeys. I constantly grumbled about the traffic and pollution. My daughter, on the other hand, would gaze out enthusiastically at the traffic to look for the policemen, traffic lights, 'bajajs' (3 wheeled motor vehicle), public buses and shopping malls along the roads. The food tasted different as they were cooked with palm oil. We prefer vegetable or peanut oil. So food generally tasted different.

Grown-ups need to figure out how to fit in. We are constantly shedding negative contemplations so we can just get going with our plans. We end up battling each day of our lives because we constantly need to adapt. Children do not make choices about where they should live. They develop an immense ability to adapt and are resilient. Many parents agree that moving houses is easier while the child is under 6-years-old.

When you have a newborn in the family, the very first thing you do every day is to check your calendar about plans you make the night before. You will discover that you are spending less time sitting around the house and getting less sleep. The days seem to go by very quickly and the nights are even shorter. By the time your child has turned 8 months old, you know this change is going to be permanent. I do believe that I have made it as far as I could because of my daughter. There were lots of sacrifices made whilst trying to figure out how to adapt and adjust.

Here is the thing. Grown-ups seek to have comfortable homes where the family can live, whereas the child lives wherever the parents choose to go. Who is better at adaptation? The child is. Needless to say, although I have reached maturity, my ability to adapt has regressed. Yet, for my child, it is the complete opposite. Our growth seems to work on the inverse proportion. The older I am, the less adventurous and tolerant I become.

A grown up, who lives abroad, never adapts his life in the same way and to the same degree' compared to a child[4]

---

4   Maria Montessori, The Absorbent Mind, Henry Holt and Company, New York, Page 62

PART TWO

Your Work Or Your Child?

That morning, I walked into the school as usual. As I was walking towards the classroom, I heard a voice calling for me softly from behind. I turned around to see who it was. Indeed, it was my director. He gestured to me to enter the classroom. We sat down quietly at the table. He was a Chinese man, tall built and bespectacled. My husband previously saved his son's life at the school barbeque. That day, his son was playing near the swimming pool. At first, everyone was watching intently at him. A senior teacher then walked slowly towards him and stood by to see what he was doing. This made us turn away and we continued with the barbeque. "Splash!" We heard it loud and clear. The boy accidentally fell into the pool. However, it was dark at that time so no one could see exactly where he was. My husband dived into the water and swam across from the other end of the pool to look for the boy. He hoisted the little child up to safety towards where the senior teacher was standing. He quickly reached down to help. As he stood up, he shouted across to us that his wallet was still in his pocket so he actually blanked out and could not think of what to do. In spite of how close he was to the boy, he could not make that decision to drop the wallet on the ground and dive in. I was bewildered.

Let's get back to the meeting in the classroom. I wondered if the conversation which was about to take place would involve this incident. After all, it was his son's life. Perhaps, he wanted to update me on his boy. Initially, I also thought of thanking him for having me at the school. I did not intend to renew my teaching contract which was ending in a few weeks' time. My thoughts flew by and disappeared very quickly as soon as I heard what he had to say. "Hanifa, I am sorry, we have to let you go. We don't think you are a good fit for our company's culture. Please pack your belongings." At that moment, my mind was a total vacuum. Between us, there was nothing left to talk about. I had taken a lot of slaps and rejections in my lifetime. When one more came right out of nowhere, you could feel that stab in the chest and the punch in the belly. It was evident that the gift of life did not count in the corporate world. When you stop becoming relevant, you are worth nothing.

Later, I found out that a teacher who worked with me in the class had made several negative feedbacks. None of the parents or students made any complaints about me. How was it possible for your co-worker to be so displeased with you that you would lose your job? She smoked when she was outside the school. Moreover, her boyfriend was the senior teacher I spoke about earlier. Do I need to say more?

There was only one reason I could think of. I sensed that she was unhappy with her life, so she took it out on someone near, me. I vividly remember her always saying to the kids, "What does 'B' sounds like?" Does sounds… She used the same question all the time. Instead of telling the head of the department, I spoke to her directly. It was unappreciated as I later discovered, she was talking so much bad things about me but never once told me what I should be doing to be better at my job. On the contrary, I got fired because of her incessant greed to feel more important.

"If that is the case, I have to take my daughter out of this school as well. How can I afford to pay the school fees?" That was my immediate response. A mere scratch on the skin but I made him realise he had lost two people, not one.

I packed up my stuff and walked out of the school. Although the school was still empty that morning, my mind was full of thoughts about what to say to my family when I got home. I had no feeling, no contempt or envy. I accepted that it was not for me to stay in this place.

On the way home, I couldn't stop thinking about how to pay for her kindergarten education. Education was always going to be expensive, more so if you were a foreigner. Fortunately, it didn't take me long to locate a new school for my child. Before I enroled her, I managed to secure a job as an English teacher at the language centre nearby. I had additionally started studying for my Diploma in Montessori Education.

One and half years went by without much drama. This company also decided to hire local English teachers as the cost would be lower. By this time, my daughter's preschool education had cost nearly USD5,000. This is the kind of pressure parents have to go through. Education has become the sole purpose of getting a job. Money is no longer used to serve food on the table or go on family vacations. I had added pressure after learning from my friend that the Ministry Of Education expected every child to have a pre-school certificate before entering Primary School. In fact, that was not true as I found out later all they wanted to know was if the child had been in our care.

A few weeks after I left my second job, I received a call from a kindergarten in Central Jakarta which was located 2 hours away from her second school. Apparently, word had gone around that I was teaching Mandarin and the school needed someone urgently. The pressure of transferring my daughter again weighed down heavily on me. Give me half the chance, I would fly out of the country as quickly as possible.

Life has another plan. It has its way of showing you how it wants you to make peace with your past. One day, as I was walking past the principal's office in this new school, I saw a lady sitting at the desk. My movement caught her attention. She turned to look out of the opened door. Indeed, it was the same teacher from my first job. What was she doing there? I had to find out. So I walked towards her to greet her. She told me she was there for a job interview. Apparently, the company was not happy with her as she was always negative and displeased with people and events. As a matter of fact, a few other teachers were told to leave after I had gone. Was it Karma or was it just coincidence? To see her sitting there for a job interview in the same place where I worked, I could not help but feel that my loss was compensated. I was at peace with life.

My daughter finally graduated from Kindergarten. However, I could not attend the graduation ceremony because I had to sit for my Montessori practical examination in Singapore.

You can choose not to work but you cannot choose not to look after your children. Wherever you go, your children have to go with you.

What Is The Meaning Of Work?

Work to an adult is the expenditure of energy to obtain money, an outcome, a result or change in the environment they live in. It is seldom a process of exploration to acquire knowledge, perhaps experience but only base on a defined need or the desired outcome.

The concept of outcome, result or change to the environment is absent in a child. The child's ability to conceptualize these can only incarnate in his mind during the conscious and subconscious periods. The child's knowledge that an activity (including sleeping) has a start and an end comes to him like day and night; it is transitory, not permanent.

Many of us introduce the phrase work after we say to the kid, "Daddy is going to work love. He'll be back to join you for supper this evening." Nevertheless, we do not refer to the tasks we do at home like laundry, sweeping, wiping, cleaning, vacuuming, dusting, watching television or even walking as work. We frequently say to the child, "Mummy is sewing the button on dad's shirt." "Dad is trying to fix the car." "Your elder sister is cleaning her school shoes," or "Daddy, would you like me to pour milk in your tea?"

It is common to use verbs or action words often with children. They are overtly spontaneous and active. That makes our communication appears dynamic. However, we seldom realise that whilst we see the activities we do as tasks, the kids regard them as work. Indeed, when there is movement, there will be work. "When a place is not tidy, there is work to be done." Maria Montessori. For us, work means an expenditure of energy in the direction of the desired outcome or results in return for monetary gains or specified goals and objectives.

Kids Work To Grow, Adults Work To Live

	Kids	Adults
Time	Endless	Limited
Purpose	Grow	Live
Reason	Grow	Live
Objective	Grow	Live

Love Of Work

Kids are not empty vessels for us to fill with knowledge, information and lots of images. If they were empty vessels, they could not have learned. They need to absorb knowledge, not to collect images, movement and sounds. There is a process of growth at work. Consequently, they are justly very much interested in doing work. They work because there lies a direct compensation for effort and time invested.

The child does not work to earn a living or fulfil an external need. He particularly repeats the same task (like washing his hands, going to school) several times but shows no hint of fatigue. Next, he feels significantly more empowered and charged with greater fascination towards his work, and continues retreating to experience work at diverse points and more noteworthy levels. In addition, he does not turn to his parents or adults around him to ask for ask favours, prizes or pay for his investment in time and effort. His motivation is intrinsic, his inspiration is inborn. And he is not even being passionate about it, he directs his activities in a way that engages in him the will to do it himself.

The child in us continues to demonstrate the same pattern of behaviour. In figuring out how to play tennis, badminton, swimming and so forth, many coaches will tell you that the path to excellence is not to be analysed, rather be experienced and practised. To love work, we have to enjoy the thought of having to repeat the task or work. This even includes, cleaning up after dinner, washing dishes, doing laundry, making beds or having a shower. So a significant number of these works we do have been rehashed typically to the point that we seek simpler and more productive methods for finishing them. The dishwasher machines, sewing machines, washing machines, and many other electrical and household appliances are developed because they render learning redundant. They can replace manual work done by individuals. Consequently, repetition will lead to the disclosure of new and better ways to do these works.

The adoration for work will likewise prompt activity of focus and a condition called self-control. Indeed, even without any reward or compensation for effort, a child is prepared to work if he or she can experience focus and concentration. Therefore, this is when we use the term 'hobby' or 'passion'. As long as the task is not compensated by a tangible outcome such as money or wages, we call it a hobby. How silly are we to fall for that dirt trap?

At this point, I would like to pause for a moment to compliment all stay at home parents with no pay or benefits. On the off chance that it was not for their adoration for work, the house is not a home. Clothes will not be cleaned and ironed, shoes will not be polished and sparkled, showers will be mildew covered and grimy, the fridge will be empty and filled with leftover from a takeaway and 3-minute noodles.

Likewise, businesses hunt for people who have encounters with work in their respective profession. When you enter your details on the resume or application form for a job, there will be a segment where you need to state your level of experience. When an expert in health and medicine appears on a talk show, his experience is reflected by his insights on the topic. Experience is why people love to work.

If we take away the child in us from the cycle of life, then we would fizzle as people. It was the child in us, who taught us to walk, talk, run, ascension, read, tune in, sing, creep, applaud, flicker, shriek, blow, lick, eat, suck, smell, touch, scratch, skip, bounce, jump, hop, jump, sit, stand, curve, nestle, love and cuddle. Figuring out how to end up children again may appear to be incomprehensible because we have gotten to be grown-ups and our developments are more liquid. Even so, we have used such expressions as 'Stop Kidding', 'No Kidding?!', "Stop being childish?", "Spoilt brat." That is just being uninformed on our part. As people who love to work, we can still learn like children if we give ourselves the chance. Our workload will be less heavy.

Listening and speaking

When the baby is 7 months old, the ears are completely formed and are ready to use. Listening is the first skill the baby learns.

After they are born, they watch how you speak from the movement of your lips and how you communicate with others. They figure out how to make sounds and begin to listen much more. After about 3 years, the child is sent to school. It is in school that the child is taught to read and write. This is the time when you start to worry because you that the natural process of learning is disrupted. You start to compare. It is not uncommon for parents to do this. With many children gathering all at one time, it is normal to want to see your child perform better than the rest, look prettier and tidier or behave more appropriately in class.

What has been your response when your child doesn't do well in school? Do you think less of him or less of yourself? On the other hand, do you start to discover shortcomings in the educational system, the teachers and other children who are in the same class as your child? You may be right about your child. Notwithstanding, this means you go through another cycle of listening and speaking exercises. Pay attention in class, don't respond to the domineering jerks, tell your teachers about it, so on and so forth. You start to notice their careless mistakes. You worry that your child is not focused and inattentive. Listen you say. Try not to talk when I'm talking.

Here is what is actually happening to your kid. The cycle of learning, from listening to speaking, is interrupted. The child is now expected to be spontaneous at listening and speaking. Furthermore, the hands, limbs and arms have to start moving and co-ordinate even faster. Therefore, the child has to adjust and adapt. The school environment is not designed to support one child's growth. The school has to arrange all classes in such a way that all children have the chance to explore growth. Consequently, it may seem that your child is regressing. In fact, the child is progressing at the most comfortable pace possible. Henceforth, you are better off following the child instead of expecting the child to keep pace with the school programmes.

Listening and speaking always come before writing and reading.

Which do you think a child does first? Read or write?

Grown-ups typically start with reading before going into writing. As a result of this learning habit, formed after leaving school, parents emphasise more reading and writing. Are you constantly battling between writing (do your homework, write your essays, learn you spelling list) and reading (study) with your child? If so, you may want to pay attention to this.

When we ask our children to read, we expect them to be reading words, like us. We therefore think that reading will lead to writing. In actual fact, we can write without knowing how to read the words. For instance, if a child is asked to write the word photosynthesis, he will start to find the image of the pattern of alphabets used for this word. He scribbles down the word that at first appears in the mind as a blurred image. However, the child will not be able to know that "ph" makes the sounds like "f" by blending two sounds together unless he has been taught how to blend this.

Another example, let's assume that you do not understand Mandarin. Try to write this sentence "我是一个人". Without knowing what that sentence means, you can still copy the strokes and form the same characters yourself. Would you agree? Ignore for a moment the strokes formation. You can tell that by looking at the character, your eyes will pick up certain patterns, which will then be transferred to your hand to start copying the lines, called strokes. Thus, writing is a process that can be done even without knowing how to read.

Consequently, writing to a child is the act of moving the muscles to make a print. The stick in the sand, chalk on the floor and paint on a canvas and patterns on a whiteboard are all writings to the child. They have no names. They are just printed matters.

Writing transforms the impressions in their minds into visual images. Children leave traces of these images by writing, scribbling or painting. Therefore, you can always encourage children to work with their hands but you cannot impress upon them to read what others have written. They can relate faster to their own handwritten notes and drawings than the nicely printed books. In this regard, you can cultivate the reading habits and writing skills, but you cannot expect these two to take place spontaneously.

One of the ways preschool teachers try to develop reading habits is by letting the children write and draw what they love. Thereafter, the children are urged to talk about their finished work of art. What they have drawn or written is the exact impressions in their minds. They will then be able to appreciate books written by other people because now they understand there is such a wonder of nature called **thinking**.

Question:

Which do you think a child does first? Read or write?

Answer:

1. Writing….in fact starting with scribbling

2. Reading…children can recognise signs long before they can write

Write Even If You Think You Are Not Good At It

I didn't realise I was not good at writing till after 16 years of school. I notice my grades had always remained above average but they were not excellent. It was until I started to write on my blog that I discovered that to be good at writing either, you need to give yourself permission to make the mistakes. To be good at anything, you have to give yourself permission to make mistakes. Skip the part about you are not good enough. Then keep on writing again, until you get to the point where you know you are ready to make a comparison between what was and is.

My website http://www.childhoodspeech.com is still at number 1 on google search engine. I have written more than 300 articles for the world to read. I am a co-author of a bestselling book. I can now compose my own talks in both English and Mandarin.

These writings are our experiences which we pen down using a writing tool. It is about what we know and want to express. If speaking comes from the heart, then writing comes from the mind. Writing is the only true expression of our knowledge about life. We scribble, draw or paint. Whenever we do things with our hands, our intelligence grows and knowledge develops. Henceforth, allow the words to flow and write.

Allow me to talk about a 10 year old kid who studied Mandarin with me for about 10 weeks. According to him, he is very slow in his regular class. However, when he was in my class, he seemed to enjoy learning Mandarin very much. He finished his classwork ahead of the top students. He might not know that he could be good at something because he was constantly comparing himself with the rest of his peers for the same subjects. As a result, when he completed the work the night before, he was very surprised with himself. The rest of the class did not do the homework. He had discovered his potential to learn. Now it is up to us to let him show us even more hidden potential through more relevant activities. Let me remind you that this is the first time this kid learns Mandarin. To be able to produce this piece of work within 5 sessions, it is simply remarkable. Brilliant.

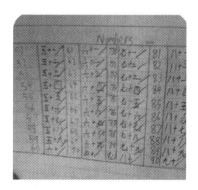

Our kids need to discover listening, speaking, writing and reading. They need us to spot their strengths. He needs us to motivate him to leave his urge to agree with "I am not good enough" to "I am going to try to be as good as I can become."

Writing precedes reading and speaking comes before writing. The most important social tool is speaking. Writing is about creating images in print about the experiences you have. In other words, when you speak and write, you are experiencing life. Allow your child to quit reading when they need to. They may be telling you they need to socialise. Test their knowledge.

Smart readers are not bookworms, nerds, geeks or 书呆子 (bookworms). They engage and socialise with the community.

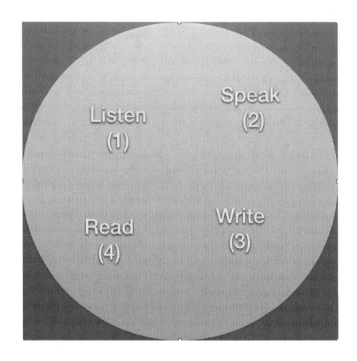

Reading

In this information age, reading has become the most dangerous activity for kids. They can read almost anything online. This means that it has become difficult to prevent your children from being exposed to bad literature posted online. Therefore, we should take due diligence in ensuring that our children know how to pick their books to read.

Reading textbooks is fundamental to learning in school. For inculcating the habit of reading, you have to set aside time to enjoy reading by yourself also. This is because children model after what you do, not what you think you should be doing. Remember that thinking is private in nature, but a movement is visible.

Encourage your children to master how to use their textbooks.

Teach your children to follow the teachers in the class by placing their textbook on the table. This is necessary because kids typically do not know how to take notes when teachers are explaining concepts in class. Therefore, textbooks are there to assist in comprehending what is said and what shall then be used for exercises.

If you worry about your children not paying attention in class, then make sure they come home with scribbled notes on their textbooks. It is not uncommon for primary school students to start writing only after the teachers prompt them to do so. For instance, when the teacher says "Copy this.", you can instantly hear the movement of the pens and pencils. It happened to all of us when we are in school. Movement, listening and seeing do not come simultaneously and readily for children that age in classes unless of course when they are playing.

If the kids have not paid attention in class and do not write notes, they will go home empty. They definitely will. There are only the temporary memory files in their brains that store the knowledge. Then they have to recall from that tiny recesses of their mind what teacher has said in class. Henceforth, if our children need to make that connection between the textbooks to worksheets, we must first show them how to make use of their textbooks.

Love For Repetition

Children's love to repeat a task or activity hundreds of times diligently is a means of satisfying a psychological need within them. They need to grow and the only way they know how is to keep repeating an exercise because they cannot comprehend instructions. They learn by absorbing images and impressions from their surroundings. Exercises like the washing of hands, playing chess, or just singing the same old nursery rhyme are often repeated. It shows they can concentrate and, in fact, ignore the 'noise' from their surroundings.

People who are concentrating on private thoughts dislike being interrupted or distracted. Grownups know that thinking is private, but children do not. When children are concentrating, their mental activities escape the observation of an adult because the activities are showed by meaningless repetition of an exercise already familiar. Swimming, washing of hands, singing and running are just some of the repetitive activities children do.

The work adults do as culinary specialists, manufacturers, artists, cooks, designers, flight attendants and pilots, naval force officers or day by day stuff like rest, shower, washing dishes, making espresso and shopping for food, are all routine! They are repetitive! How often does an American Idol hopeful need to sing to get noticed by the voters? How many times do our parents have to nag at us to tidy up our room for us to learn that we are unkempt? What number of driving lessons do we need to take before we are entry to a driver's permit? Repetition is not uncommon in the lives of grown-ups.

So how can we even judge a child's work as **meaningless repetition of an exercise already known?**

The answer my friends lies on how much we value the exercises we perform. Children do not repeat their exercises to achieve an external aim. They have to develop from inside. Adults more often than not think of their external objectives, like paying bills or feeding the family. Furthermore, we are subscribed to the demands of our livelihood. Accordingly, we have to perform.

How To Love Repeating Doing Work?

To understand how this works, I need you to answer these two questions. What are your life values? What do you value that provides for you?

Value

When an individual values life, he wants to protect it, in the same way he protects his children. The whole basis of what becomes important to him in life is the value he gives to his worth. Unfortunately, for many other individuals, once they have achieved the targets, they forgot to revise the value.

Attitude

Many people still adopt the "look and see" attitude when it comes to learning. This is the "line and sinker" attitude. There is no hook. You look and see. You want to find out more before making the commitment. Without a hook, you do not stand a chance of getting any fish. You can lure people to teach you things. Knowledge without practice equals no experience. The only reason I can think of about people who learn this way is that they have no idea who they are as a person and do not respect or value the work they do.

Many of our daily routines are repetitive. Doing the laundry, washing dishes, taking showers, brushing teeth, talking and walking. If we enjoy doing the work, the work itself become valuable to us. If it rains heavily today, you will not be able to take a walk. You give 'walking' value. If you are love having a neat and tidy house but you have fallen sick, you will be frustrated and restless. You may consider hiring a part-time maid. What we value most, we will pay to keep the work going even without us being there. Work becomes a job or business that carry a monetary return. It is not the money we earn per se that defines work. It is the value we attach the work we do.

Work

Develop the habit of loving repeating your work because when you repeat work, your value increases. Your experience multiplies and you will be worth more to others who value the work you do.

Long Life Learning Principles.

1. From Instinct. If you learn from instinct, you will fear failure. You will act instinctively to protect and save yourself. You become quick at making choices. If you are about to cross a busy road, you don't think. Although you stay careful and alert, you do not have the time to think. You act with courage and clear vision that you want just to get across safely. You hold your child's hand tightly. Instinct will get you and your child across. This is the lowest level of protection that the animal species are given. *

2. From Intuition. My first teacher on parenting is my single and unmarried self. If that person wants to go out for a drink with a friend, the parent in me says, "I can't. I have to look after my daughter." If that person wants to spend an extra 10 minutes facing the mirror to finish combing my hair, the housewife says, "Later, go and pick up the laundry before the rain falls." Everything I want to get done instinctively for survival, I respond by intuition. It is sometimes impulsive, at times, so scattered I feel proud that I can be silly.

3. From respecting who you are and the values you want to serve. Keep yourself grounded so you can be accountable and grow to become authentic and responsible for the work you produce. You will become matured in the delivery of your services. You will figure out how to be happy and contented without compromising the happiness of the people you serve. The whole purpose serving people is to exercise your sense of freedom to make choices. How can I deliver to help improve the quality of other people's life? Where can I get the resources to improve myself so I may inspire, motivate and lead? I need to be the best, so I will only do what I know I am best at.

*Why Affirmations do not work.

Do you believe that telling yourself "I can" does not work?

"Whatever the mind can conceive and believe, it can achieve." Napolean Hill

That works.

By saying I can, you are consciously trying to override what you disbelief. Your alpha brain (the conscious mind) is diffused while your beta brain (the subconscious mind) is forced to work.

The gamma (the awakened mind) and theta brain waves (deep meditation and light sleeping) are dormant. Your subconscious mind is sleeping. If you only "Start With Yes", but your subconscious mind is not ticked to work, you are forcing yourself to work on overdrive. You will fall sick, depressed and after that you start to hate the process. You now believe you are not good enough.

HACK!

Metaphysics is undeniably more than just left, right and blind spot. You need to study how your brain functions, while you are still strong. Find out how to maintain a high level of energy.

Those who have prayed and cried in the spirits, and I do mean that which causes you to kneel down on both knees and prostrate. You are in a state of desperation; you are too weak to think, too feeble to move and too confused to speak up. The pain you are experiencing is beyond description. It is not only an excruciating pain because it is a stabbing on the chest. All you can do is cry from the soul.

Have you been through depression or recovering from one? You may relate to this. Even as the family room is watching TV, you are modestly participating, smiling ever so lightly as if tickled by a comedy act. Furthermore, you have this impression that people are staying away from you. They see nothing wrong with you because you are a master in the art of disguise. You seem so normal standing next to them. They say you are quiet. In fact, it is the best you can do for yourself because you heart is hollow. Hollowness is your only companion as it offers you clarity. Life outside of your body is indeed confusing, scary and not dependable. In your final analysis, you agree that you have lost your resilience, grip and footing.

Subsequently, your life takes a downward spiral. It has reached rock bottom. Instead of waiting to hit the bottom of the pit, you resign from yourself. Fortunately, a sense of purpose still lingers in some fragile veins. The blood jolts a nerve that has yet been numbed by your senselessness. Why are you worrying about what other people say anymore? You are about to lose your life by your own hands.

Are you following me so far? If a friend needs to talk to you, ask this question, "How is your day?" Give your friend 5 minutes of your precious time. It is as simple as that. On the other hand, if you are the person who is depressed, please pick up the phone and dial the number you can remember quickly. Don't be choosy or selective about whom will talk to you. You may even be surprised that your worst enemy does not want to hear that you are depressed. Your alpha, beta, gamma and theta brainwaves can no longer serve you. You concede that to save yourself from committing self-harm, you can only depend on your instinct. That is the basic principle of survival we talk about. That is the lion's roar, the snake's venom, the scorpion's sting and the skunk's noxious spray. Your instinct will save you.

Affirmations do not work. Now you know why. They are not strong enough to keep you withstand the blows that life will bring. You need prayers, reminders (Zikir in Islamic faith), supplications and meditations.

Beta brainwave performs what your alpha cannot. By itself, it is not a medium to affirm your belief. It will not be enough to say yes because you are still not changing. You're merely sabotaging yourself.

When you have reached the end of the rope or just about have enough of the difficulties, you must use your instincts. "I can?!" Instinct will keep you alive. "I cannot?!" Instinct will set you free. You will use whatever it takes to get back on your feet and live again.

Love For Details

Children have amazing eyes for details.

Have you ever have children coming up to you occasionally to point out the light speck of dust on your face? Or the small paper in the corner of the room? Are you amazed at the wonder of how children work with details?

Do you notice this about your child? Children have an amazing pair of eyes for details. Sometimes when we pour too much or too little water in a cup, they are the first to point it out to us. And when you have a tiny pimple on your nose or an ant on the table, they too will be staring at it for the longest time.

This is a characteristic of the child that is so simple and pure. Start following your child and if you see this truth, you will become more patient with your child and with yourself too. You will wait for this phase of growth to play its part to shape your child's intelligence as he or she investigates how things work in this world and how associate names with things, people and places.

Modulations Of Language: The Adult Can Learn Again

All the characteristic modulations of languages are best acquired at a young age, preferably under the age of 7 years. It becomes clear to us that adults who are learning a foreign language that they are carrying the imperfections characteristics of his native language or mother tongue. So how are you able to help yourself to succeed in learning something new? After all, all theories and argument of languages seem to point a fact, it is better to start learning when we are young? Logically, you won't want to waste time deepening your knowledge even if it was to help your child. You concede that you have passed that age.

We can revisit our inner voice, the inner child and use the same natural powers endowed upon us since our birth for our continued growth.

We have taught ourselves to walk, talk, sit, crawl, turn, jump and skip for more than 6 years without formal training. If you revisit those moments, you would probably not even remember the steps of how it had happened. This is because the child's growth is intuitive. If the child was handicapped, he would know how to use only the limbs, organs or senses that were usable.

Just as we had corrected ourselves when we were just 2 years of old. By looking at other 2-year-old children, you can make reference to your personal experience. You were the toddler who had tried to take the first few steps or grip a pencil. Indeed, you had the power to authorise this highly intuitive child to learn. We are capable of correcting our imperfections which we carry into our adulthood by using this intuitive learning process.

All kinds of movement we have ever learnt were first performed by the child. Well, before the adult comes along who decides to speed up the learning process by all sorts of theories and new practices, the child was there first. Call it what you like. "Go back to basics", especially when the spiralling effect of speed learning or leap learning is beyond reach or becomes confusing.

You may be interested to know that many religious converts who embrace a new religion as an adult learn the scriptures in whatever language they are given. How is it that a Westerner like Cat Steven could suddenly say a few prayers in Arabic when all his life, he only sings and speaks in English? How is it possible that millions of people who do not speak Hindi love to watch Hindi movie and then sing in the same Hindi language? Or a Malay person speaking Japanese and singing in Tagalog?

Indeed, the power to speak, write and read come from our inner teacher. This inner teacher is the same child who was your body's master. Be willing to revisit your childhood. Explore and taste the life of a child again. The experiences will help you overcome many of the fears you are now facing as an adult.

Concentration

I have been asked this question many times in so many different ways about focus and concentration in studies.

- How do you get your child to focus and concentrate?
- How can I get my child to focus on his studies?
- How do you make a child study?
- What strategies do you have to get a child to sit down quietly to listen?
- How do you get your child to do the things you need to get them to do?

How Does A Child Act?

A child's impulses are spontaneous, thoughtless, uncoordinated and unplanned. However, they can always be seen playing quite happily despite the fact that they lack planning, coordination and technique.

In a controlled or prepared environment, for instance, at a swimming pool or gym, there are rules and conduct of behaviour to be followed in these venues. The purpose is to protect the safety of the children and also adults. So you may find those children who are unable to abide by these safety rules and regulations annoying or distracting. On the other hand, they behave perfectly fine outside a controlled environment, Why so?

Children are little social creatures like the adults. However, they seek social qualities like companionship, love and admiration, respect, reciprocal help and moral support beyond social organisation. "These are facts so delicate and refined that a spiritual microscope is needed to discern them, but their interest is immense, for they show us the true nature of man." (*Maria Montessori, The Absorbent Mind, Henry Holt and Company, New York, Page 228.*)

If, in the society of children, we are already seeing self-control, self-love and care for people of their own kind, what can we learn about children who are learning to focus and concentrate? Indeed, they lure them by constantly moving. In their constant toil to reach the norms of behaviour, they act to arrive at that level which we come to describe as normal.

Indeed, normality is such a favourite word that we attach our own definitions to it. For our children, they are outcomes from growing up. Whether you call it normal or not, it makes no difference to them. Their work is to grow, not to seek growth of any form. Consequently, we must never set a prelude based on their unorganised structure, rather create possibilities and opportunities to support them and get them to as far as their energy and growth can take them.

How can you bring these opportunities to them? The answer is quite simple. Share them with the rest of the world. Do not hold back. You can give money, food and time. These are basic to survival. You will find a way to get them. But you can neither give knowledge nor experience. Firstly, children are not empty vessels to be filled. Secondly, you cannot buy knowledge and experience. When you learn, you get knowledge. If you use knowledge, you get experience. So, share your life knowledge, your experience, time and space with children. Give a little at a time because growth is a journey. Enjoy the process.

The upshot from this is that your child will begin to trust the process. It will lead you to follow the child more readily. We will discuss this topic 'follow the child' in a later chapter.

Love Of Silence

How are we to understand the real meaning of silence if it were not for the presence of noise? You have finally come to the section on "love of silence". It is the most enchanting characteristic of the child.

On a cold winter night, the fireplace in the family room at home would be the perfect place for sharing the quiet ambience of the night. A candlelight dinner, a lullaby whispered through the ears of an infant, a gentle sway of the waves on the lake as the pelican glides through. We can be totally enveloped by the beauty of the environment and the warmth of loved ones which silence brings to us.

Silence is mandatory in the recording studio for voice over, dubbing, newsroom and recording artists. If it were not for silence, the quality of the voices will not be captured in the recording.

Most crimes are plotted and planned in silence. Even though many crimes are also committed in crowded places, criminals attack quietly. Animal predators like lions hunt by staying silent, prepare for the lunge before pouncing on their preys. When the conditions are perfect for the kill, the criminals are transfixed in silence.

Silence is not a word that can be taught. It is like thinking, always private but never revealed with gestures or body language. In other words, silence is not naked. It is an experience, not an experiment.

An incidence of silence with a baby may go like this. A baby is sleeping silently in the mother's arms. You can the baby breathing and moving ever so gently, wriggling elegantly. An elder brother, still just 2 years old, watches on and is drawn into the picture of silence. The baby continues to move but stays laying in the protective arms of a mother. At this point, mum allows the boy to lay a finger on the baby's palm. He laughs because the baby squeezes the finger. With silence, the other senses are stimulated. The child learns from this experience what silence means and registers the lesson in his mind.

Silence is a condition of life in perfect harmony with its environment; a sound can be heard, but it is noise. Silence capture the beauty of nature to a picturesque view of the landscapes, the green pastures and hilly mountains.

In case you are wondering if a child needs noise to be entertained, consider two of the most popular silent movie stars and comedians: Charlie Chaplin and Mr Bean. They draw the best out of the child in all of us. We laugh from our bellies. Or perhaps you may watch Just For Laugh Gags. I don't remember ever hearing dialogues in the skits. There is music but there is no dialogue. They connect with the audience all over the world in silence.

To honour or remember of people who have died, we stand in silence for a minute.

Exercise

There are two ways to teach silence, the first one is what I have learnt in my Montessori course and the other is my own. I have worked with both successfully.

1. Montessori method: Before you present this picture, write the word 'SILENCE'. Show a picture of a lake or a mountain. Ask the child to look at it for a few seconds. Then ask what they see. After that, flip the picture over to show your child the word.

2. Childhoodspeech™ method: Use a kitchen timer from Ikea. Turn to the dial to 5 minutes. When you release your hand, you will hear the ticking sounds of the timer. This is the only thing that the child should be listening to in the room.

Both methods have helped my students to arrive at focus and concentrate quicker. They can be applied together or in isolation. I find the kitchen timer is effective for time-sensitive tasks like doing examination papers or training self-discipline. For example, if I turn the dial to 40 minutes to rest, it means I give myself only 40 minutes of resting time. When the time is up, the alarm will go off. Because there is a soft ticking sound coming from the dial, our attention is transported to focus and concentrate. The sound stimulates the senses and commands movement.

PART THREE

Follow The Child

I had the rare opportunity to observe my daughter while I was studying for my Montessori course. She was about 4 years old at that time. This was the beginning of my 'follow the child' experience. I was the observer, facilitator, admirer and follower of her growth. I wrote down her conversations, kept track of when she first started playing the piano.

When we admire our kids' talents, it can only mean one thing. We are inspired by their growth. Inspiration is the process of being mentally stimulated to do or feel something, especially to do something creative. It gets you moving towards your goal. Mentally stimulation sums up the whole process of us wanting to follow and join the development of a page, program, celebrity chef or entertainer. Stimulus is the key to action. Our children, no matter what age they are, constantly look for things to do to stimulate them mentally, move them physically and uplift them emotionally. It is the way of a growth, it is a joy for them. If they cannot get stimulated at home, they will seek action outside.

So it is essential for us to be inspired by our children. From the time when they latch on to us for breastmilk to the day they are able to walk and talk, we constantly look for the little new changes. It is called the phases of development. We observe and follow.

What Do You Follow?

Having been online blogging since 2008, I noticed an interesting thing about the do-follow and no-follow in HTML coding. I will not go into details of what an HTML is. Briefly speaking, when you are building a brand and you post a link, with a "no follow" command in your HTML code, you retain authority on that click. Dofollow links are links which we want search engines like Google, Yahoo or Bing to follow from our page, and Nofollow links are links that we don't want bots to follow. Usually, whenever we have to link to any bad domain, we use no follow link attributes. Interestingly, this led me to connect "follow the child" with what people do when they like pages on social media posts.

When we like a post on Facebook, Instagram or LinkedIn, we click the like and / or follow button. We instantaneously tell the system to store our subscription to that link that posted the page or picture. Then the system starts to send you the latest posts automatically. Unless you stop following, you will continue to receive updates.

Imagine this, why do you click "Like" unless you are fascinated or interested to cast your vote? You are 'inspired', otherwise, why do you follow?

So understand this. If we could have a list of all the things that your child has either followed or liked, you would have a comprehensive list of the things they are inspired to do. That's exactly what Facebook, Google, LinkedIn and every social media are getting out of your child. Your child gets involved in social media because they only receive relevant and interesting updates. These relevant and interesting updates have been based on what have been liked or disliked. Social media companies know more about your child than you do.

Imagine having this list of stuff your children liked to watch and listen to on the internet, would it not be easier for you to know the ESSENTIAL things to provide for your child?

The reason why we lack an understanding of how to communicate with our child is because we stopped being inspired by the child.
– Hanifa K. Cook

The reason why we lack an understanding of how to communicate with our child is because we stopped being inspired by the child. It is a reflection of what we resent in ourselves in our childhood. We then tell our children what we do not like about what they do. For example, wearing short skirts, girls talking to boys, talking on Instagram, being on social media. We fear for them. We fear losing control of our children. When fear takes over, we question them. "What are you doing?" "Who are you talking to?" When we stop seeing the growth, we stop admiring, we stop getting inspired and we literally stop being creative. The future starts to look more like a distant hope. We cannot look beyond the actions. Aspirations will die. We will stop following the child.

Parenthood lies in this very basic principle, 'follow the child'.

Imagine if we could help our children close that gap between interests and aspirations even more by knowing how to help them achieve their aims. Imagine if we could track down every single likes on all the social media platforms we have used from Instagram, LinkedIn, Facebook, Youtube and Twitter, we would have relevant information to create targets and achieve these aims.

Inspirations And Aspiration

Aspiration means a hope or ambition of achieving something. Turns you away from your past and make you look towards the future. Inspiration is the process of being mentally stimulated to do or feel something, especially to do something creative. It gets you moving towards your goal.

When you are inspired by what your child does, you will follow the child, as you would as a fan of famous and popular individuals.

When children inspire their parents, parents aspire for them too.

Exercise

Discuss your children's aspirations with them.

PART FOUR

Live Up To Your Parenting Potentials

Have you hurt yourself as a child? I was playing catching with my siblings and neighbors. Our playground was made of concrete and sand. The slides are made of concrete, smooth concrete slide. Everything there was made of natural steel, wood, cement and sand. A bit like Gaza but more fun. It was a happy place. The see-saw was made of real metal and a great wooden plank. It was one giant obstacle course. I fell down hard on the ground and a small pebble stone hit my left shin and got stuck in it. I saw my flesh after rubbing the stone off. The skin was ripped apart. The flesh turned from white to red. Then I started to cry.

When I was well again, I went back to the same playground again. The joy of playing was better than the pain I had felt. I was a child.

I can see the scar. There was the pain but I laughed at the way I cried. I sat down on the ground and cried out like little Tarzan. The entire neighbourhood must have heard me. My late aunt (bless her soul) carried me home. Then she nursed me. That was me. I did things that would hurt me. But I was a child.

How Can You Learn From Your Childhood and Be A Confident Parent?

Why do some people find it so difficult to produce a piece of work? Is it an unwillingness to get started or an innate feeling that they are just not good enough to do the job properly?

Remember the times when your parents asked you to help bring in the laundry from the clothes line? You looked at your father and he didn't seem to be doing anything anyway. So why should you? Or your father asked you to help to take the garbage out. You looked out the door and said, "Well, the truck won't come till the next morning."

You don't seem to get it. You couldn't take the first step. Just do it. If only your parents had been more persuasive, for an instant, "Let's take the garbage out or bring in the laundry. We can clear up the room faster if you can help out."

You will notice something about the way parents "ask" you for help around the house. Sometimes it's almost like begging. Parents don't like delegating the job to their kids. In many cases, when you were asked to help, your parents are exercising tough love on you. They are building character in you. Be responsible, dependable, trusting ....All that you want for yourself and your children.

I know for certain that thoughts of our childhood and how we have been brought up will always be discussed and shared amongst family members all the time. When I am alone, I will recall those days when I had to help out with the dishes, cleaning the floors or going to the grocers. These memories do not just leave your system. They surface in your mind like bubbles. Why not start making use of that information and harness them instead of pretending it is a forgotten history. I have reiterated in the earlier chapters that childhood experiences do not leave us. It is we who leave childhood because that is how we grow.

So if you want to conquer your fears or worries about parenting, here is what you can do. Take an instant in your childhood where your parents would tell you to do things around the house, like closing the windows or making your bed. Do you think that you now make your bed because it is part of your work as a homemaker? I think not. It is part of the nurturing process that have gone into parenting. Our parents have been telling us to do the work over and over again for years. So much so that it helps to remind us to overcome laziness, procrastination and self-doubt. Parenting is mostly repetitive.

Parents don't teach us to be lazy. This is a fallacy. Supposing a child does not get to do any housework, do we say that the child is pampered by the parents? Perhaps so but, that is just an opinion open for discussion. Indeed, it is also highly probable that parents do not want to see their child doing the work they are supposed to complete.

Consequently, if you're feeling really lazy, useless and hopeless right now, remember that our parents have been kind, in fact too kind to us. We should get back up and start living up to our parenting potentials, no matter what. There is not a chance of losing or failing in parenting unless you stop trying. If you have failed in in examinations, marriage and business before, it has nothing to do with parenting. Your chid did not sit for your examinations, marry your spouse or run your business. Get on with it. Your parents are waiting to see you with a smile on your face that you are managing without them beside you. Everything is going to be all right.

Parents never set their children up to fail in life.
Your childhood experiences can provide you with a wealth of
knowledge and support to build your confidence in parenting your
own child. Use these experiences to empower and motivate you.

Don't Worry, Be Creative

The only way to break free and leave behind your worries is to get creative. Creativity changes the path of worry. It helps you change focus. Let me ask you this simple question. Why do you worry?

1. You don't have all the right answers to your problem.
2. You do not know how to help.
3. You don't know where to begin although you do want to help.

The day I decided to get up from the hospital bed to feed my daughter, my worries went away. I was on morphine because I was in pain after my emergency caesarian. After therapy, I managed to get out of bed. The thing that I worried about was that I would not be able to withstand the pain again if I tried to get up. But when I thought of my baby girl not getting any milk from me, that worry just went away. Where is the creativity in that?

Have you ever seen a baby trying to roll itself on the bed or crawl? The baby learns by creating movement. So instead of lying in bed worrying, I started to move. I took a deep breath and in one swift action, tightened my belly and turned. I found a way to stop feeling the pain.

Creativity does not come from having the right answers, knowing how to do or knowing where to begin. It starts from a movement in the direction to change your position more towards fulfilling your true intention. Don't just stand there and watch. Don't just sit there. Don't just this. Don't just that.

So what will you do today to get creative? Change your current state. Move.

PART FIVE

Parenting Pearls

10 golden pearls for your personal development in parenting.

1. **"I am not afraid not to be liked by my children."** Create boundaries, principles and lay down the ground rules. You are the parent.

2. **"My child is a gift for me."** Treasure your gift with smiles, hugs and kisses. They say plants grow well when you talk to them pleasantly and regularly. So does your child. Be inspired by your child. Be inspired by how your child transforms his learning. Embrace change as the child grows from a baby to becoming an adult.

3. **"My child walks a different journey and I will be there to walk together with my child."** The child needs facilities to grow. The child leads a journey that will be totally different from yours. You may have experienced how you can play the winning game in life. You have led yourself to achieve. You have pushed boundaries. You have made that big leap. You hope that your child will follow your style in the winning game. That is not going to work. The child is not you. The child does not have to take on big challenges like you. You live a life different from your child. So how can your child experience the same kind of growth? While you're at work,

your child is sitting for the examinations. While you're walking home from the market, your child is writing the last question to the mathematics paper. Remember that growth is a process, not a destination.

4. **"I accept failures and mistakes."** Failure is not a mistake. It indicates to you that you have to refocus your attention. Every step your child takes is a necessary step to rediscovering how to use better tools for future tests and exams. Anyone who tells you that they can bake the perfect bread every time is lying. Success is made up of mistakes and pitfalls, which may have turned into a mountain of trash for you to walk on and climb to reach the top. You still have to take that climb. At least you did not throw your rubbish in another person's backyard.

"My parents don't give up" - this hold true to my own family too! Just an hour ago my 18yo son shared his Yr2 / 1st term results and said "I feel like crying - for the joy but also for the grave mistake I made for 1 module - wrong submission, I could have scored 3.4 instead of 3.18! Learning from this grave error! Lucky me I manage to cross the 3pts GPA!" Well, I did remind my son... I have never given up on you, even with or without progress as long as you learn well from your learning journey! Mistakes are meant to happen to let you learn more and you will progress and leap further! Identify and analyze what went wrong - plan to best manage and level up further for next term and move on!

- Masayu Nurjannah, parent and member of #ipostforparents on Facebook

品德高尚

品德: The bright side always covers the dark. You can choose to be bright but that's not all you are. Darkness is vulnerable, it is beautiful. Brightness is glaring, it is charged. Vulnerability is where energy is stored. That's why the stars shine the brightest at night.

That's why if you look at the word 口。it's means a mouth. It's an opening. There are 3 of these 品 。it simply means an article. With 德, it means moral character.

Your moral character reflects how much of your dark side is used to bring out the brightest part in you. Loose the nerves, there's potential energy stored in that darkness. When it's your turn to shine, yes, when you shine, check it out, everyone can see you.

5. **"I do not apologise for my absence with a gift."** Do you buy movie tickets to make up for the time you didn't spend last weekend because you're busy at work? Or do you buy ice cream because you miss his concert? That's not a treat. That's an apology! Do not compensate your absence with a present. It can never bring your child closer to you. It only bridges the gap between you and your child. When the bridge comes down, the gap remains.

6. **"I am always ready to be vulnerable."** We do become vulnerable in front of our kids, don't we? Spilling the tea, standing in front of the kitchen door while calling out, "Dinner's ready", walking out of the shower room with hair yet uncombed, our heads talking, "I better check on our kids if they had their shower or breakfast." When you are vulnerable, you are actually holding on to potential

energy which when released in the right direction, will take you to a higher level of confidence and self-esteem. When you are nervous, you send off the energy in all sorts of directions. You lose your sense of purpose and direction. Know the difference.

7. **"I cry because it cleanses my soul."** We speak strong and cold to get what we need because it helps to suppress our struggles, only to feel more vulnerable later.......Pause, I have managed to stop doing that. Then there are times we have to cry. That is normal, is it not? It is impossible to grow without shedding a tear in your lifetime. It cleanses the soul. Sometimes, my daughter watched me and she would put a hand on me. That touches me deeply. Then she whispered, "Mum." She lays her head on my lap. We have grown to the norms of a society, called the adult norms. There is no other way to grow except from within ourselves. As my body starts to become less able to do the things I could when I was younger, I seek to rest, reflect and learn even more about myself.

8. **"I only say I cannot when I need help or I am willing to learn to do it."** Learn NOT to say to yourself "I cannot" unless you are willing to learn to do it. You will find a person to teach you or learn to do it somehow. There are Mandarin translations to "I cannot":

我不能 not able to
我不可以 cannot
我不行 not capable of doing, cannot
我不会 don't know, cannot

In English, "cannot" means "cannot". In Singlish, "like that" means "like that". In Chinese, it's more than that. What is cannot?

"Cannot" means I don't know but I won't ask for help. Many people stop short of reaching out for help when they say "I cannot". Don't skip this step. You're obliged to ask for help when you say "I cannot".

9. "I have a support system in my parenting journey. I do not walk alone." A nucleus family consists of a father, a mother and a child. Surround yourself with people who can support you in your journey. Join parent support groups in your schools, speak to teachers and principals, talk to your parents about how they see parenting, share time with other parents to share your experiences with one another.

10. "I select freely, choose wisely, decide willingly and live courageously. I am able to give love unconditionally and receive love abundantly." 在生活里，往往会遇到挑站。时时刻刻要学如何做决定， 好的决定， 必将会带你往前走 。

> 乐意去挑选
> 做出智慧的选择
> 愿意决定
> 勇敢地奋斗
> 争取成功
> 梦想成真

Our Goal As Parents

Our goal as parents is to raise a child who
never has to recover from childhood.

How Am I Inspired By My Child?

I am inspired by my child because of the unique approaches he takes to solve all life's problems. He shows me that there are a lot of ways to solve one problem and you can see things from different angles, therefore, gaining different insights.

Jo Chung
Owner and founder
www.colourfengshui.com

Last July, My husband & I sent our 11-year-old son together with 5 other children his age for an exchange programme in Fukuoka, Japan. Many family members thought we were crazy to let our son go on this programme because it was the month of Ramadhan and he would be spending five days in Syawal with his Japanese foster family. It was a tough decision but we wanted a different kind of education for him. I was also hoping that my son would pick up Japanese. Although he could not learn much in 2 weeks, I was inspired by his determination and endurance. While preparing for the trip in June, he had actually fallen sick. Despite his condition, he still managed to learn the Japanese language and culture, and even attended the dance practices. He has made us very proud of him especially when we saw him live on YouTube performing with his friends.

Norhaiza Yep Abu
Special Education Teacher

My Helmi came home yesterday giving me a hug telling me: "Ibu I did it! I have progressed between 10-35 points for all my subjects! I passed with better grades for my Mathematics!" He was full of smiles. I have left him alone to do self-study. He has not only learnt to manage his time, he has progressed at his own pace! He is beginning to learn and pick up the skill set of a self-directed learner, just like his elder sister and brother. I'm impressed and inspired by my Helmi He had scored very badly for Math and spelling. Yet he has never looked back but stayed focus to progress.

Masayu Nurjannah
Loving Mother of Three Children
Herbal Specialist

I have three children, each of them having the strength and weakness which are different from one another. I am inspired to manage my time skillfully by juggling between my personal goals and helping them achieve their goals.

I want the best of everything for them. I register them in schools of our choice. I am willing to fork out money to pay for them to learn additional skills such as learning to play the piano, guitar and do ballet. I ensure my children are well equipped and ready to face tough competition in the future.

I am aware that I should not rob them of their childhood. They will perform well, enjoy childhood and possess good moral values. They achieve these by having a balanced lifestyle. This task is monumental for me. But I am committed to putting in the effort, managing my time well and accepting the support from the community.

Ir. Turisina Ramli, MBA, CIDTT, Int'l dipl. Montessori
Director of Studies Indonesia Montessori and Indonesia Persada Gemilang

My days are filled with hundreds of significant tasks for two demanding children, a 5-year-old and an 8-year-old. I have school runs, drop offs and cleaning up to do at home. The most stimulating conversation is always having to explain why the lights should turn off at 7.30 p.m. and homework should be completed before the weekend starts. Plus I have to explain to my expatriate neighbours why my children have more tuition classes than theirs.

Such is the gruelling academic system in Singapore. You trade sleep for dark circles. To save the trips to the hair salons, you cut your hair short to a bob or tie it into a ponytail. You have quick showers. You have nights that end later but days that start earlier. You carry school bags instead of designer handbags. Your house resembles the aftermath of a major hurricane, with worksheets, assessment books, textbooks, nerf guns, Barbie dolls and so forth strewn on the dining table. The list is endless.

When you walk into the kitchen at the end of the day, you know you have enough of the mayhem. These are the days when I could barely lift up my head. I just need to lay down on the bed. It becomes daunting to think of having to go through another day.

Alas! I still wake up for my children every morning. Ironically, they give me the strength to carry on. The inspiration seeps through my body and fills it with energy. It pulls me towards a centre and grabs hold of me from within. I begin to smile with satisfaction and the sense of achievement and contentment. You love your children unconditionally. So they love you too, need you and depend on you. They do not have to know how to tell you. These messages come from their eyes.

When I am old, I will look back and laugh at how I am overcoming these challenges now. I will smile then because this is the parenting journey, a meaningful one.

Sharifah Nurasiha Almaghbouly

Testimonials And Reviews

My personal development for parenting and business supports my desire to support my family to progress regardless of the odds we have to face. I am evolving myself and embrace change. I particularly enjoy the discussions within the Facebook group, iPostforparents and reading the blogs at http://www.childhoodspeech.com. Your insights as a devoted mother and a business person have fostered the close relationship with the members. I have indeed benefited from this experience! First, I learn to be a better parent by coaching my 10-year-old son in his school work using your Childhoodspeech™ and FollowTheChild principles. The blueprint has helped Helmi & I to learn and explore new techniques to revise his school work more efficiently! Helmi loves your session and will definitely apply them.

You have also patiently guided and helped me to be a homegrown Herbal Specialist. I am confident that your good work will help many parents and business owners to shine!

Masayu Nurjannah

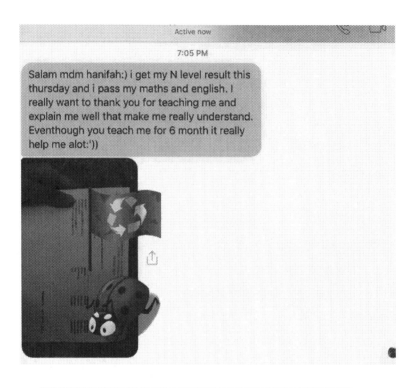

Active now

7:05 PM

Salam mdm hanifah:) i get my N level result this thursday and i pass my maths and english. I really want to thank you for teaching me and explain me well that make me really understand. Eventhough you teach me for 6 month it really help me alot:'))

Muhammad Nur Mohideen Thank you so much Hanifa K. Cook for your guidances. Words cannot express how i felt. I always believe in Sumayyah Nurfatihah ability.

Muhammad Nur Mohideen
Father Of 10 Children
Preventive And Curative Advisor

I strongly believe that every parent who is in business should pursue personal development. Building a business from scratch while managing family commitments can become a roller coaster ride if one does not know how to strike the right balance. The guidance and tips that Hanifa shares in her 'iPostForParents' Facebook group are extremely valuable gems that help us to reflect and make our lives better. Her new book will be an inspiring read.

Jasima Syed Sulaiman
http://www.FussFreeEditing.com

To Join Facebook Group, please visit
http://www.facebook.com/groups/ipostforparents

Printed in the United States
By Bookmasters